SOMEWHERE INSIDE a MIRACLE

How God Breaks Through
When Hope Seems Gone

Emily McCoy

Somewhere Inside a Miracle
by Emily McCoy

Copyright © 2025 Emily McCoy
All rights reserved.

Printed in the United States of America
ISBN: 978-1-962802-28-4

All rights reserved. Except in the case of brief quotations embodied in critical articles and reviews, no portion of this book may be reproduced, stored in a retrieval system, or transmitted in any form or by any means—electronic, mechanical, photocopy, recording, scanning, or other—without prior written permission from the author.

This work depicts actual events in the life of the author as truthfully as recollection permits and/or can be verified by research. Occasionally, dialogue consistent with the character or nature of the person speaking has been supplemented. All persons within are actual individuals; there are no composite characters.

Unless otherwise noted, all scripture is taken from the New American Standard Bible®. Copyright © 1960, 1971, 1977, 1995, 2020 by The Lockman Foundation. All rights reserved.

Scripture quotations marked NASB 1995 are taken from the New American Standard Bible®. Copyright © 1960, 1971, 1977, 1995 by The Lockman Foundation. All rights reserved.

Scripture quotations marked ESV are from The ESV® Bible (The Holy Bible, English Standard Version®), © 2001 by Crossway, a publishing ministry of Good News Publishers. Used by permission. All rights reserved.

Scripture quotations marked NIV are taken from THE HOLY BIBLE, NEW INTERNATIONAL VERSION®, NIV® Copyright © 1973, 1978, 1984, 2011 by Biblica, Inc.® Used by permission. All rights reserved worldwide.

High Bridge Books titles may be purchased in bulk for educational, business, fundraising, or sales promotional use. For information, please contact High Bridge Books via www.HighBridgeBooks.com/contact.

Published in Houston, Texas, by High Bridge Books.

Contents

Introduction 1

1. Blake 5
2. October 27 15
3. Little Hope 23
4. The Miracle 31
5. What's Next 39
6. New Normal 47
7. The Good Shepherd 57

References 69

Introduction

I have become a marvel to many,
For You are my strong refuge.

—Psalm 71:7

I DON'T KNOW HOW MANY HOURS OF MY LIFE I have spent in car lines in front of schools. Let's just call the sea of cars my second home. I have tried over the years to make good use of that time, as it is a significant chunk of my afternoon every school day. Like a waiting room experience followed by that rush of making dinner, getting to Haidong Gumdo (Korean sword fighting, if you're not familiar), and cramming in homework once we leave the parking lot chaos. From the driver's seat of my car, I have written Christmas cards, assembled scrapbooks, chatted with family members on the phone, and yes, even changed diapers during some seasons of life.

But the most beautiful thing that has come from this time has been quiet conversations with God. Sometimes, I peacefully pour my heart out to Him. Other times, I tearfully plead my case and ask for guidance. I have a habit of praying aloud, so it's possible that I'm known by the other parents in cars around me as the crazy lady in the red van who regularly has very emotionally charged conversations with herself, but hey, I'm alright with that.

In fact, it was in a car line, very late in my pregnancy with my son, Benjamin, wedged between my seat and the steering wheel, that I prayed Psalm 71:7 over him. I prayed he would be a marvel to many because of what God does in his life. I'm not exactly sure that I had a detailed plan for how that would go. Just that he would be. The dismissal bell rang, and my daughter came out to the car. Moving on. It was one of those prayers that I would soon see God undoubtedly answer, and even though I didn't have precise expectations, how He answered was absolutely beyond anything I ever could have fathomed.

I will say now: This story is very raw. It's a testimony of a brutal walk down a path no parent ever wants to travel. My story can be a difficult read, especially if you have had a similar experience. The pages ahead are a full-disclosure-kind-of-honest look at infant loss and navigating the path of a child with undefined special needs. Our family's story includes joy and bona fide miracles, loss and sorrow, and many things in between.

I know that I'm not remotely the only parent to walk this route. But that's exactly it. I'm not writing this because I've faced things no other parent has. Many parents have gone through a road like mine, or maybe your circumstances are very different, but you've stood in the same shoes of desperation and confusion as the world around you falls apart. That's why I'm telling my story. God has comforted me so that I can comfort those in any trouble as I have been in (2 Cor. 1:3–5). For this reason, I have also added a chapter at the end of this book called "The Good Shepherd," which takes a bigger picture look at infant loss, prebirth and after birth,

Introduction

and includes some of the tender things God has revealed to everyone in His Word and used to heal my broken heart as I walked that road.

At the beginning of each chapter, you'll notice a Greek or Hebrew word with its definition. Nerd alert: I really like definitions. During the 2020 chaos, we all needed to find ways to cope with the added stress that came with that season. One thing that helped me keep my sanity was studying Greek and Hebrew transliteration (putting their word sounds into our alphabet to make it readable in English) of Bible passages. You're dazzled. I can see it on your face. *Everyone* wants to be my friend once I tell them that. Okay, really, more like "party of one," but nonetheless, what began as more of a curiosity became a passion of mine. If you're hoping to do the same, I recommend BibleHub.com. I hope someday to be able to read actual Greek and Hebrew fluently, but I'm certainly not there yet. I'll keep you posted.

What inspired me was that the definition of the Greek/Hebrew many times paints a much more colorful picture in my mind than the English does. You may not relate to being an amateur etymologist, and that's perfectly okay in my book (pardon the pun), but throughout my family's story, I've woven in a few language tangents for you in hopes that they will bring that deeper, much more colorful meaning to your mind and heart as well.

Ready? I'll walk this with you. Come on, let's go.

1

Blake

*eggizó (Greek): to make near, to come near
... expresses "extreme closeness,
immediate imminence—even a presence"*

Before diving into Benjamin's story, let's rewind a few years to a point in my life when God used some unnerving circumstances to align my heart with the next part of His plan. Our family had just made the move from Ohio to Texas, and we were enjoying our new life in the South when I began having a host of symptoms that were both familiar and out of place at the same time. I was nauseated all day long, exhausted no matter how much I slept at night, my sense of smell in constant overdrive, and I was uncharacteristically moody. You can probably guess what thought was formulating in my mind as the root cause, and once the thought of pregnancy takes up residency in your brain, it leaves room for little else.

Hands shaking and heart racing, I took the big test, confident I would see that life-changing word, and—nope.

Several negative tests left me feeling confused, as these symptoms just weren't subsiding. If anything, they were becoming more problematic. I could barely stand the thought of food and began to worry about what could be causing this if not pregnancy.

I shared my list of woes with my mom, a nurse practitioner because, still to this day, she has an almost perfect record of being right about what's wrong. Thankfully, this was one of the few red marks on her record because she warned me that I might have ovarian cancer. However, even then, she wasn't too far off target. I hastily began pursuing imaging with my doctor, and long story short, I discovered I did, in fact, have a rather large mass on one of my ovaries, which, by God's grace, was benign but needed to be removed due to size issues.

The feeling I had after solving the riddle of my symptoms surprised me. Despite being elated that my diagnosis wasn't cancer, I was equally disappointed that I wasn't pregnant. I found myself still hoping. At the time, we had two beautiful daughters, Emma and Ashley. We were happily living as a family of four. My heart and my calendar were both full, caring for the girls I was already raising. Sure, I had toyed from time to time with the idea of having more children but had never felt like someone was missing from our family, and I had certainly never shared my musings with my husband, Pat. We were, after all, in a different phase of parenting at that point. Our girls were eleven and nine. No more messing with naps or diapers, baby gates or car seats—you get the idea. Dare we venture back?

I wanted to. It was more than needing a "baby fix." God had taken a desire that was a small flame and poured gasoline all over it.

After surrendering my heart to God in prayer over and over, I decided to talk to my husband about the matter, thinking he would be less than enthusiastic. To my surprise, he was delighted by the idea as well. A longing became a plan, and a plan became a positive pregnancy test several months later.

This time around, I was considered a "geriatric" pregnancy, and yes, I was a little older (35), but I feel the word geriatric is a little harsh. So much had changed since my pregnancies with my girls. Instead of waiting for my first OB appointment to know my due date, I could now visit sites with due date calculators and week-by-week updates on what's happening inside. Because I am a planning nerd, I had a baby name book ready and waiting. The meanings of names have always been a fascination of mine, so to me, this was not a chore at all. I was underlining and marking from the day we found out.

One name was special to me before the search began: Noel. We had chickened out using it twice, but if we were blessed with another girl, I was not going to chicken out a third time. Before, I had thought, with my girls being born in August and October, that Noel would be a little too Christmassy. With my due date in July, nowhere near Christmas, it wasn't an issue for me this time around. I'd missed my chance before and wouldn't again.

I will never forget my first doctor's appointment, not as long as I live. My new doctor routinely did ultrasounds at the first visit, which I wasn't prepared for but was overjoyed to see our new baby, who would resemble something like a jellybean at that point in early December. The image appeared, and I beamed at the sight of my new blessing. Then I heard my doctor's compassionate, somber words.

"Your baby is smaller than it should be right now, and I can't detect a heartbeat. I'm so sorry."

The reality of what she had just said suddenly fell over me like a heavy blanket. My baby was already dead. I'd had no physical indication of a loss. She told me I was experiencing a "missed miscarriage," which is when a baby's life ends, but the mother's body doesn't respond how it normally would to a miscarriage. She told me we could do more ultrasounds to be sure. She said many things after that, but I heard very little.

Already dead? And I didn't even know?

I don't remember driving myself home. I know I did, but I was operating completely on autopilot. All I remember was coming home, thankful that the house was empty, and falling on the floor of my bedroom, screaming. Some of that screaming was directed at God: "What do you want from me?!"

In the middle of my ranting, I heard my phone chiming text alerts and then ringing with a phone call. I knew without looking that it was my husband, wanting to know the blissful details of my first visit. There was no way I was going to break the news to him while he was at work. I'd just felt the sting of being blindsided alone, and I didn't want the same for him. Once he realized I was avoiding answering texts and calls, he came home, and I dolefully told him that our little jellybean was already gone. We just held each other and wept.

We hadn't told many people at that point that we were expecting, but we did have to break our news to some family members. I found myself afraid to tell some of the people who knew, not just because it was a difficult thing to share, but because I feared they might say something that would make matters worse. Some people, perhaps with good intentions, attempt to answer the question of why things happen, or while trying to lend comfort, end up belittling the pain that's anything but small. Graciously, when we told them, we were met with support from the few friends and family who knew.

The next week was honestly tormenting. I had scheduled a second appointment with my doctor to see if we could possibly hear a heartbeat after waiting a few more days. That week seemed like months. Was I still considered pregnant if my baby wasn't alive? Cruelly enough, because my hormone levels hadn't changed, I was still dealing with first-trimester nausea and fatigue, which is a different animal when you know you're enduring miserable symptoms without a happy ending.

The normal Christmas cheer that fills December felt like anything but. Melodic lyrics in the Christmas carols on the radio that I would gleefully sing along to during any other year became bitter mocking reminders of the dead baby I was carrying. Peace on Earth. Baby in a manger. Noel. That one hit the hardest by far. I tried busying myself with writing Christmas cards, a tradition I typically enjoy, but what on earth do you write in such a situation? Most of the recipients had no idea what was going on, and I felt it best not to share.

The day of the second appointment finally came. I didn't have high hopes that the verdict would be much different. We looked again at a tiny baby the same size as a week ago with the speakers turned up as loud as they would go to hear any possible trace of a heartbeat, but all we heard was the steady hum the speakers made. I never knew silence could be so deafening.

I was glad my doctor repeated what to do from there because I had absorbed nothing the first time. There were procedures that could do what my body wasn't doing naturally if I wanted to go ahead with those. For now, I could wait, but not indefinitely. I chose to wait as long as I could. Even though it was clear by now that the baby was no longer alive, I didn't want to look back later and wonder if things would have been different had I just waited a little longer.

About two weeks later, on December 23, my body finally physically miscarried at home. Although I knew it was coming, I was still so unprepared. Most of all, I could not bring myself to part with our tiny baby. I knew I could not keep my baby the way I wanted, but discarding him or her in any way was unbearable for me. Not long before, a friend happened to have given me a small turquoise ceramic box with a decorative cross on the top, which had since been sitting out on an end table in our home. It was the only thing that brought me any peace to put our baby in. Pat and I decided to bury our baby's remains, just the two of us. Hollywood could not have set the scene any better. It was cold, dark, and rainy outside as we said goodbye to our precious child before we ever got to say hello.

Not knowing whether you lost a son or a daughter is a cruel thing for a parent to endure. I prayed for years following losing our baby that God would affirm whether I had lost a son or a daughter or let me see my baby in a dream. Even before my physical miscarriage happened, I decided I couldn't handle referring to our baby as "it," so we decided to choose a name for our baby. Not knowing whether to choose a boy name or girl name, we looked through gender-neutral names and chose Blake as the name our baby would have.

Picking a name brought a small amount of healing for us. A pain unique to loss through miscarriage or stillbirth is that the list of things you will never do with your child includes absolutely everything. You'll never look into their eyes, see them smile, or hear their laugh. There will be no first day of kindergarten or high school graduation. The one sacred thing we could do was choose our baby's name.

The next few months were emotionally tumultuous. I had worked through the first stage of grieving (denial) before I had physically miscarried. After that event came the next stage: anger. I tried going to our gym to find a physical outlet for what I was feeling, which helped until I started getting a little too much attention from one of the employees. I didn't feel threatened, but I wanted more than anything to come, work out, and go from the gym anonymously, and this guy just wouldn't let that happen.

Since the gym wasn't an option anymore, I tried making an extra effort to get out of the house regularly while the girls were at school, but pregnant women seemed to be absolutely everywhere I went, so I found myself staying home more than usual, which only left me more inside my head. I asked myself questions that I knew there were no answers to. What did I do wrong? Why were other mothers' babies fine, but mine had to die?

I was also dealing with a lot of confusion. I was sure having another child was the path God had set us on, so how could losing our baby have possibly been His plan? I wrestled with whether or not I could bear trying to conceive again and, in doing so, risk going through loss and grieving all over again. My gut reaction was no. There was no way I could lose another baby and not be destroyed by it. I wasn't even going to try.

This is where Jesus met me. He came near. One of my favorite New Testament stories is in Luke 24: "The Road to Emmaus." Two of Jesus' followers are traveling on a road, downcast and hopeless after the recent crucifixion of Jesus, in whom they had put their hope. And for what? He is dead. It is over. Now what? That's when Jesus comes near and begins walking by their sides. He keeps them from realizing it's Him until much later when they are having a meal together, and He then leaves their sight. In verse 15, the Greek word for "drew near" is *eggizó*, and it describes how close Jesus was to His followers. As close as the air they breathed when they were sure He had left forever.

Jesus came near after I lost my baby. Though it was not a joyous time, it was an intimate one. When my prayers to Him were filled with tears and rage, He accepted them. When I doubted His plan and complained, He listened. When I just couldn't say a word to Him, He stayed by my side. He didn't just give me strength and courage; He *was* my strength and courage.

I faced trying again.

We were able to get pregnant again, but this time, we faced our experience with a different set of emotions. Pregnancy after a loss is very different. Scheduling my first doctor's appointment made me panic. I obsessively monitored, heaven knows how many times a day, to make sure I wasn't bleeding. Pat and I found ourselves using phrases like "if the baby comes" instead of "when." We informed our girls of the pregnancy, figuring it would be difficult to hide from them, but, unfair as it was, pleaded with them not to tell anyone else for the time being.

We never made any kind of social media or mailed announcement; we just kind of waited for when we couldn't hide things anymore. Conversations got a little humorous once I started showing, as people tried indirectly bringing up the topic of pregnancy in conversation, afraid of committing the ultimate faux pas of asking a woman if she's pregnant when in fact she's not. That one's a tough one to talk yourself out of. Occasionally, I would decide to disclose the reason we hadn't been forward in telling anyone, which was graciously met with sympathy and understanding.

Appointment after appointment, my doctor assured me that everything looked great, but that still didn't settle my unease. Every time she checked for a heartbeat, my own heart began racing. Feeling our baby boy move inside me once he was big enough strengthened my faith that he would be alright—until I hadn't felt him move in however many minutes. I agonized over things that had not even crossed my mind during my pregnancies with our girls. Was my placenta in the right place? Was it bad that I wasn't having much nausea? Sadly, much of the time, I lived in a silent panic.

The following December, almost exactly a year after finding out Blake was gone, Sean Patrick arrived two weeks early (true McCoy fashion). Only when I saw him and heard his cry did I burst into tears, realizing we had another baby. It didn't dawn on me until that moment how much hope I had not dared to allow myself during the entire pregnancy. Now I was gazing into his big brown eyes taking in the world for the first time. Once we took him home, there was barely a moment when someone wasn't cuddling the little guy. Christmas, while it still brought with it some painful reminders, had a very different tone this year. We were sleep-deprived, coffee in hand, walking on air. Having Sean in our lives was a gift from God after the storm we had endured. Little did we know a ferocious storm still lay ahead.

2

October 27

alalétos (Greek): inexpressible, too deep for words, unspeakable, unutterable, which cannot be uttered

WITH SEAN NOW IN OUR LIVES, WE WERE ADJUSTing to our new normal. He arrived not long before COVID, so I use the word "normal" loosely, as he wasn't the only major change. I was caring for a newborn but, like parents everywhere, also found myself suddenly managing entire school days. The loft in our home became a middle school, elementary school, workplace, and feeding and napping headquarters. Honestly, I think the girls enjoyed being able to take snuggle breaks with their new baby brother in between classes. In all the chaos, we found a new rhythm as a family.

We gained a newfound perspective by not taking for granted the many firsts and special moments with Sean. All the moments we grieved not having with Blake, we cherished with Sean. First smile. First laugh. Crawling and then walking. Hearing him coo and babble.

We cherished the more grown-up moments with our girls as well, doing our best to make things like starting middle school and high school special during the worldwide upside-down season. I discovered that having both an infant and teens forces you as a parent to be more intentional about spending quality time with each child, especially with my girls. I had to make sure that not every moment with them was overshadowed by nursery rhymes, feedings, or napping. Being that much more intentional made moments with them that much more special.

When Sean was about 14 months old, Pat and I asked ourselves, "We're done with the new baby thing, right? *Right?*" To my shock again, both my and my husband's sentiments were "no" despite not being anywhere near Sean sleeping through the night. We prayerfully considered and once again tried for another baby. If you'd say this puts us cleanly in the "crazy" category, then you'd be right, but I promise this cycle only goes so far. So once again, we celebrated a pregnancy, this time a little more hopeful than the last.

This pregnancy was very textbook, as was the delivery of our new baby boy. With each of my pregnancies have come requests from friends and family members as to what day they would like me to give birth. I've always found this a little ridiculous. "Can you have the baby on a Saturday?" Or "Such and such a date is my birthday. How about then?" Not at all how the process works. In fact, our newest blessing arrived on October 27, the most requested day for him *not* to come. One of my daughters had an orchestra concert that day, and the other had her first Haidong Gumdo belt test. I attended neither because I gave birth at 1:15 that morning,

October 27

two weeks early again, to our little man weighing in at 8 pounds 9 ounces, the biggest of all my babies.

Now, normally, my husband and I are plan-ahead kinds of people. With our other children, we had settled on a name for each gender by about month three. Not so with this one. We knew we were having another boy, but for some reason, we just couldn't narrow down the list of names. I was leaning toward naming him after one of the tribes of Israel. Judah was a top contender for me, but Pat didn't seem quite sold on that name. Once we saw him, Pat said he was clearly Benjamin, so that settled it. Benjamin Gregory, he was, with his middle name being my dad's namesake. I think the delay in naming him was God at work because the name we finally landed on ended up suiting him better than we could have imagined. Having just been through quite the ordeal, our new little guy was very hungry, so we had a quick feed, and then he peacefully fell asleep in my arms.

As I was being wheeled down to our recovery room, the nurse asked us if we wanted to keep Benjamin in the room with us or if we wanted her to take him to the nursery while we both slept for a little while. Not ready to part with him, I voted to have him in the room. Since he had only ever been inside of me or in my arms, down the hall seemed excessively distant. Pat, however, persuaded me that we needed some sleep, so they took Benjamin to the nurses in the nursery. It was one of those decisions that didn't have a right or wrong, but what we decided ultimately ended up mattering greatly.

After a brief period of sleep, a nurse came in to take my vitals and help me to the bathroom. We were making happy conversation when another very somber woman came in the room and stood in the corner. Very bluntly, she said, "I have

— 17 —

some bad news about your baby. He turned blue. The nurses revived him, and he turned blue again…" In that split second, I waited in horror, sure that she was about to tell me that my son was already dead. "They revived him a second time. He is on a ventilator in the NICU."

The nurse who had been helping me fabricated tissues from out of nowhere as I began sobbing and gasping in disbelief. Joy had instantly turned into shock and despair.

"He has to be okay; he has to be okay," I mumbled over and over, fearing that his life was going to be over hours after his birth. We were with him minutes ago, and he seemed perfectly healthy. How had he gone from that to not breathing in that short a time span?

Moments later, the nurse was wheeling me to the NICU, Pat striding next to me. We were taken to Benjamin's bedside to find him with a ventilator covering his face and tiny probes just under his skin all over his head. The NICU staff did their best to inform us of what was going on. He was having continual seizures and would stop breathing every time one came. Why? They were doing everything they possibly could to figure that out.

The ventilator was breathing for him for now, but he was not "breathing above the ventilator." It was then that another terrifying realization hit me: I couldn't hold him. He had tubes and wires stuck on him everywhere—he had to— but what was helping him live would not allow me to take him into my arms. What if I never got to hold my son again?

I did my best to stand next to his bed so I could stay near him. Having only delivered him a few hours before, I was pushing myself harder than I should have, but this was the only way to be with him. I held his tiny hands and stroked his warm little tummy and spoke to him. He moved and made a muffled squeaking noise every time he heard my voice. Monitors showed each assisted breath he took, and I glanced at them obsessively, mentally willing those numbers to change. Swallowing glass must hurt less than this.

Not long after we got to the NICU, our sweet baby was wheeled in his bed to a room for more imaging, and Pat and I returned to my recovery room while we waited. On my bedside table were hospital papers for new moms about the importance of skin-to-skin contact after birth. Guilt nearly swallowed me alive. On my phone was a text from my daughter wanting to know how the baby was. *God, please don't make me do this.*

After imaging, the doctors were able to give us a little more information. Benjamin had bleeding and swelling in the right hemisphere of his brain. They still were not sure why. They determined Benjamin needed to be transported to a Level 4 NICU at another hospital nearby, which would take place in a few hours. While I made no objection externally, the thought of being parted threw gasoline on what was already a raging fire of panic inside me. He was leaving—I wasn't. I hadn't been discharged, and while we decided that Pat would go with him instead of staying with me, I was terrified that this was the last time I would see my son alive. What if he dies before I get there? The scary part was that my usually irrational fears weren't irrational this time. They were a very real possibility.

The transport team arrived in the early evening. I was parked in a wheelchair as close as I could be to the foot of his tiny bed, giving them room to work, my face mask completely soaked with tears and snot from hours of crying.

I will never forget the compassion of one of the team members transporting him. She noticed my distress and asked me, "Have you been able to hold him yet?"

"Just in the delivery room," I managed.

She then explained that she would let me do the job of one of the transport team members and hold Benjamin while they reconnected all his monitors and ventilator to the transport unit they had wheeled in. I don't know this woman's name, but I will remember her gift to me as long as I live. I held Benjamin, his little fuzzy head against my cheek. Although time was of the essence, I think the team was slightly less efficient than they could have been, allowing me a few extra minutes with him.

When the same woman finally came to take him, I gave him one last kiss through my tears. She leaned over and whispered in my ear, "Take off your mask and give him a real kiss." Another gift I will cherish for the rest of my life.

I slipped off my mask, which was soaked beyond doing any good but was an absolute requirement in a sterile environment. I kissed his cheeks and his head one more time. "Goodbye, Benjamin. Mommy loves you."

I watched the unit leave until he was completely out of sight. A silent nurse wheeled me back to my room where I was completely alone. No husband. No baby. My sister, knowing my situation, had sent me texts, pictures, and videos of all the day's events I had missed with my girls. A wonderful concert by my gifted musician, complete with pictures of her in her orchestra dress holding flowers. A successful white-to-yellow belt test for my little martial artist. I watched in an effort to cheer myself up. Normally, this day would have been a joyful day for so many reasons. Instead, despair covered me like a blanket as I sat alone in my hospital bed. I

October 27

wondered if Benjamin was still alive. I had already lost one baby without knowing when it happened. I vividly remember thinking, *This will never be okay.* I tried praying, something that usually flowed from me. But there were no words. The pain was just too deep. Too searing. Too bottomless for any existing words.

The word *alalétos* in the Greek means "inexpressible, too deep for words, unspeakable, unutterable, which cannot be uttered." That description certainly applies to the pain I was feeling in that moment. But glory to God, that is not the only thing beyond words in times like this because He provides grace. Romans 8:26 says that "…in the same way the Spirit also helps our weakness; for we do not know what to pray for as we should, but the Spirit Himself intercedes for us with groanings too deep for words."

The Holy Spirit is praying on our behalf in all arenas of life. He's not just filling in words that we struggle to find. The pleading He does on our behalf is too deep for words of any language we could speak. Words, as helpful and necessary as they are, sometimes just fall short. Our Holy Spirit's cries for us never do. He breathes them from depths we can't comprehend, and they rush forward in coming to our aid in ways we could never ask for.

I had cried for hours and been awake for almost two days. I had given birth that day, but that seemed like more of a detail compared to the major life event that had overshadowed it. The day of my son's birth had felt more like a week. I was exhausted and numb. I wanted some sound to keep me company, not wall-to-wall silence. Desperate to break the silence, I started a movie on my phone. One of the first options that popped up was the movie *Speed*, so I went with that. If you're not familiar with the film, let's just say it's a movie about people on a bus, and something *really* bad is going to happen if the bus slows down. Interesting choice, I know. Especially in the middle of my own life-and-death situation. Sometimes things that seem like an unlikely fit tumble into our stories and end up being special reminders later. More on that in a coming chapter. For that moment, I was relieved by something besides stillness in my room. With puffy eyes, I watched until I finally drifted off to sleep.

3

Little Hope

tsalmaveth (Hebrew): death-like shadow, deep shadow, distress, extreme danger.

My husband came back early in the morning, hoping I would be discharged before the typical hospital stay of one or two days. He had learned a few more pieces of information from being with Benjamin at the other hospital and now had the unbearable task of breaking heavyhearted news about our baby. Pat, as gently as he could, explained to me that Benjamin had a blood clot, a large one at that, and it had been there for a significant amount of time. How long exactly was anyone's guess, but his brain had actually formed around it. The blood clot was deep in the right hemisphere, and surgery was not an option.

"He'll never have a normal brain," Pat lamented, tears defying his effort to hold them in. Sorrow filled my heart, and my own tears spilled out of my eyes once more. Pat's mind was in a very different place than mine. He began thinking aloud about how we could have an elevator built into our home since Benjamin would likely need a wheelchair. I wasn't that optimistic.

Amid all of this, I was served discharge papers to fill out. If you've ever done this, you know what most of the questions are about. The main concern is usually screening for postpartum depression. My honest answers on paper looked very dismal. Am I feeling down? Have I had any crying spells? Do I have any thoughts of despair of any kind? Two thoughts screamed in my mind side by side: *I need to be with my baby **now**,* and *They're **never** going to let me out of here.*

I did my best to annotate my answers with the reasons why all my feelings were extreme. Really, I'm sure the hospital staff already knew and understood. In fact, in the situation we were facing, feeling no fear or distress probably would have been more of a red flag as far as my mental state was concerned. Still, that didn't assuage my feeling like a caged animal.

My obstetrician came back to the hospital after hearing what happened. She hugged me as I tried to relay to her all that had taken place in the past day. Due to the circumstances at hand, she said that she would be willing to clear me for early discharge. Without hesitation, I accepted, not sure if I was physically up to leaving or not, but that was beside the point now. All that mattered was getting to Benjamin as quickly as I could.

It was strange to be leaving the hospital without our baby. The usual celebratory parade anticipating baby's first car ride and journey home was simply my husband and I quickly and quietly slipping out, hoping there were no questions along the way. If you've ever given birth, you know what a task it is to move with any speed in the days following, but I was giving it my all.

As dire as things still were, I was grateful to arrive at the next hospital to find my son still hanging on. I got to hold his tiny hand and talk to him, at least for that day. His head still had probes sticking out everywhere like a mane of multicolored hair, measuring his brain wave activity. As far as the seizures were concerned, he was on the maximum dose for multiple anti-seizure medications, and they were not enough to stop anything. His breathing would stop with each one, respiration only supplied by the ventilator.

Benjamin was going to have an MRI that day, and before he was taken down for his imaging, the hospital chaplain came to visit. Pat was gone at the time, so he asked me about how both my husband and I were doing. In that moment, I knew what to answer for Pat because of the man my husband is. Pat has a very strong protective drive, really in any role. It's what made him a powerful offensive lineman in high school and college. It's what makes him go outside when tornado sirens are wailing and stand between his family and the storm, as though he could stop a cyclone from getting to us. It's what keeps him from sleeping whenever he's away on business or when one of the girls is staying the night at a friend's house.

I simply told the chaplain, "When he doesn't know how to protect us from something, he's lost." He'd never been so lost before. I think the chaplain could plainly see the distress on my face, so he didn't press much into how I was doing. He prayed with me before leaving, and I thanked him through my tears as Benjamin was taken for his imaging.

I met an entire new team of doctors, nurses, and other hospital staff that day, and each of them seemed to radiate compassion. They offered tissues, hugs, pillows, and anything they thought we might need. They also provided a little flat felt doll that all NICU babies had in their beds. I was told to tuck it inside my shirt for a little while so that my scent would transfer onto it, and then they would keep it in Benjamin's bed with him. Newborns are born knowing their mother's scent, and knowing he could sense it even though I couldn't be with him was just as calming for me as sensing it was for him. Since he was on a ventilator to breathe, the nurses spread the little felt doll right over his face so that it would be as close as possible.

While the NICU staff embraced my outpouring of emotions with grace, showing this much emotion in front of this many people was very different for me. I know I have been very vulnerable through most of this book, so this may sound strange, but by nature, I'm a very private, introverted person. Those closest to me would likely describe me as quiet or even-tempered, so ugly crying in front of everybody, including the guy working at the coffee kiosk in the lobby, was very uncharted territory for me. (If you're reading this, coffee guy, I hope I didn't make you quit your job. Thanks for the coffee.)

Not long after our arrival, we were given a room just outside the NICU for us and for visitors. As parents, Pat and I were the only ones allowed to go back to the NICU with Benjamin. This room was an immense blessing during the time we needed it. It was a small room with chairs that pulled out into beds, end tables, and an attached private bathroom with a shower. As grateful as I was for this haven, part of me knew why we were getting this room. I dreaded the answer, so I didn't ask.

Pat and I had to wait until the next morning to speak to the pediatric neurologist about Benjamin's imaging. Before meeting with him, some other NICU doctors took us aside to a separate room to show us the images and explain some of the details before we met with him. If I live long enough to forget my own name, I will still never forget the images that were seared into my mind that day. The right hemisphere of his brain was pushing his left hemisphere so that the usually symmetric divide was off-kilter due to swelling from the blood clot. They used words for parts of his brain, such as "calcified," that I didn't think could be used to describe a living person's brain.

How had Benjamin survived even this long? I leaned against my husband, mostly so I wouldn't collapse on the floor.

"Do you have any questions?" one of them asked after describing the horror we were looking at. None that they could answer. I just moaned.

With tears in her eyes, one of the doctors said the neurologist would further explain Benjamin's prognosis, but at that point, we knew what it would be. Benjamin could not survive with a brain in this condition. Our baby was going to die.

The meeting with the neurologist only confirmed what we suspected. Encircled by doctors, a social worker, a family relations support worker, and several others, we were told there was little hope for our baby. His swelling was spreading throughout his brain, and his seizures were getting worse. They described outward signs of brain death that Benjamin was already showing. He was in death's shadow, or deep shadow, *tsalmaveth*, as described in the famous 23rd Psalm.

In short, modern medicine and the best professionals there had reached their boundary of what they could do to save our son in just two short days. Odds? We were given none, just options for hospice care, whether to keep him in a hospital setting or to take him home. *Hospice.* There is nothing on earth that can fully prepare a parent for the death of their child. Pat and I felt the weight of the fallen world in that moment. This was never going to be okay.

In a voice that really didn't sound like my own, I asked the doctor if Benjamin was suffering. I couldn't bear for him the few days he had to be in excruciating pain. The doctor assured me that Benjamin's medications were keeping him from feeling pain. I'm sure a trained MD can see signs of discomfort in a sedated patient who cannot speak, but I could not wipe the terrible feeling from my mind.

After the devastating meeting with the doctors, Pat and I retreated to our room and held each other and sobbed. We began the grueling process of calling family and friends, some of whom were still expecting a joyous update on our newborn baby. One call after another, we recounted what had happened and heard hopeful voices break into hysterical cries.

When we returned to Benjamin's bedside, there were no longer probes cascading from his head. The doctors had learned what they needed to know. The blessing in this was that it made it easier for us to hold Benjamin in our arms, seated just next to his bedside, as he still had a ventilator. Pat and I spent the rest of the day and late into the night holding him. Kissing his little head.

I told him about the places we would have liked to have taken him to. How I wished I could take him to the beach and to the beautifully painted mountains of the Southwest. I wanted him to see how breathtaking a sunset can be, to run barefoot in the grass, and to catch fireflies. I wanted him to jump into an icy swimming pool on our hot Texas summer days. I wanted to take him to see fireworks and animals at the zoo. I wanted to go with him to the theme parks my parents took me to as a child. I told him about all the things I wanted to teach him to do. I wanted to know what his smile was like and how his voice sounded. I wanted to hear him laugh and wipe tears from his eyes when he cried. I wanted to read to him while he sat on my lap. He was going to miss these and a million other wondrous moments.

I told him all about his sisters who had been anxiously awaiting his arrival. How he would have had to grow up with a mom and essentially two assistant mothers, which would have meant the poor kid wouldn't have been able to get away with anything but would have been loved on every minute of his life. I told him about his brother who, at this point, didn't understand that he was getting a younger brother but needed him terribly. I could barely utter the words to tell him that he had a precious sibling, Blake, who was already waiting in heaven for him, no doubt ready to run freely with him in a world so perfect that words here on earth cannot describe it.

I told Benjamin about his grandparents, how my parents had raised me and how Pat's parents had raised him. Pat's mom, as well as many great-grandparents who had gone before him would be waiting for his arrival as well. I told him about all the extended family still here that he would not get to meet, at least, not for a long time.

We cuddled him for hours and hours, going through box after box of tissues. He enjoyed being held close, nuzzling as best he could with his ventilator still spread tightly across his face. I tried to imprint on my brain how his soft skin felt, his warm little head against my cheek. I wanted to remember his sweet little smell, the soft little fuzz that his hair was. I wanted to remember those little things as vividly as I could, knowing I would live the rest of my life trying to recall them. Pat and I stayed with him until we could barely stay awake, but it just wasn't enough. Given the circumstances, what would be?

4

The Miracle

haptó (Greek): to fasten to, lay hold of, cling, i.e., (specifically to set on fire—kindle, light

THE FOLLOWING DAY, THE HOSPITAL ALLOWED US TO bring visitors back to see Benjamin, as they do in end-of-life situations. It was our desire for my parents to be able to see their grandson, even if only for a moment. We also gave our daughters the option to see him, understanding if that would just be too hard. At that point, they knew their new baby brother's prognosis.

We had also called Broc, one of the pastors of our church who handled the care of weddings, funerals, and other life moments. We contacted him, knowing we would have to start planning a funeral soon, hoping he would have some guidance he could send us. We didn't ask him to come to the hospital, but he dropped whatever it was that he was doing and was there in minutes.

I will never forget sitting next to Benjamin's bed with my daughter, Ashley. She had been crying all the way to the hospital with my parents, but she later told me, "When I saw Benjamin, I was just happy." I found out later that she, even as a germaphobe, refused to wash one of her hands for a while because it smelled like Benjamin. She held her baby brother and talked as fast as she could for as long as she could.

What broke my heart was that everything she said to him was in complete faith that he would be home with us in a few days. She advised him that Daddy was willing to pay money for catching flies in the house (an offer my husband has regretted ever since) and suggested that Benjamin could make extra money by leaving doors open for a few moments to allow flies to come in. Not that she had ever done anything like that. She gave him all the dirt she could on their siblings and what he could expect from them. The line that most melted my heart was when she told him, "I know you don't know right now how big the world is, but God has the whole world in His hands."

Being held up by the faith of your children is a truly humbling thing. I would love to say that my faith was steady and brazen through this trial. It wasn't. Just like Peter who, commanded by Jesus to step out of the boat, began sinking because he took his eyes off Jesus, I was looking at my own metaphorical waves, and I had never seen waves like these. My daughters, however, fully believed that their baby brother would come home.

This wasn't the first time their faith had truly humbled me. Indulge me in a lighthearted reprieve for a moment (perhaps you need one right now). My daughter Emma has always loved dragons. They have always just been her thing. When she was little, she used to pray for a dragon nightly. She would ask me if I thought she would ever find one. Not

The Miracle

wanting to crush her dreams, but also not wanting to give her false hope, I would diplomatically say that if there was a dragon to be found, then God would show it to the ones who ask Him and then, in faith, begin looking for it. If you're a boring, unimaginative adult like me, you might suspect that I had no faith at all that anything of the sort would ever be discovered. I hoped that maybe God would show her something maybe more conceptual, as I knew her childlike prayer was still heard and still mattered to her heavenly Father.

Fast forward several years to nobody's favorite year, 2020. Emma was in middle school and had long since stopped praying to find a dragon. It was then that we stumbled across a news story on television, and to my utter disbelief, a headline heralded a recent discovery in Canada of remains of what scientists were calling *Cryodrakon boreas*, or "frozen dragon of the north." There was a picture of what this beast may have looked like while still alive, and I just sat with my mouth gaping open at a complete loss for words. Now, did this big guy breathe fire, guard treasure, and do all the other dragon-y things in fantasy tales? Likely not. But I looked over at Emma, who was doing her best to play it cool, and there was no hiding the smile on her face.

In that moment, the faith of a child had put me in my place. I felt sheepish for not having an ounce of faith that God would answer her prayer. I believed He created the entire universe, that He parted seas, that Jesus performed miracles of all kinds and even rose from the dead. But I was too "grown up" to believe He would answer Emma's request with anything mind-blowing. I could feel God asking me, "Did she ask Me for a *concept* ... or a *dragon*?"

The same way that Emma's child-like faith humbled me then, Ashley's faith was more than humbling me now as we presented a much more earnest desire before God—that He would heal our son.

After our family's visit with Benjamin, Pat and I took a break to eat breakfast and to spend a moment alone before what we believed would be our son's last day on earth. We would be taking him into Camp Christopher for privacy instead of staying in his NICU bay. No ventilator. My mind struggled to wrap itself around the thought that he may that day go from being in our arms to being in the presence of God in a single moment. Would he still be a baby there? Would he be a little boy once he got there and go from ventilator to running through heaven's fields in a matter of a few hours? It's one of those mysteries that we won't know this side of heaven.

My husband asked if I was ready.

"I'll never be ready for this."

I didn't know if I was about to see my baby struggle, and if so, for how long. We had walked the painful road before of being at the bedside of a loved one taken off life support, and it was a brutal experience. To be honest, I was angry that we were being asked to endure it twice in a lifetime.

I am forever grateful for an amazing woman named Elizabeth who walked this harrowing road with us. She was one of the NICU nurses at the hospital and was caring for Benjamin that day. I don't know how you prepare yourself as a professional for a day like the one she knew she was going to have. She was an utter godsend of quiet strength on a day when we had never needed it more. Before taking Benjamin to Camp Christopher, she prayed with us over Benjamin.

The incredibly ironic thing about that moment is that when I look back on it, I see it as a moment of joy in its very definition. It had nothing to do with the outcome of the day. I didn't expect a good outcome. In that moment, I had the peace that comes with knowing that this was not the end for Benjamin, even if he left the world that day. I knew beyond a shadow of a doubt that the moment he left, he would be in God's presence, fully alive. And even though I wanted a lifetime with him first, I knew that this would not be the last time I would be with my son. I would see him on the other side of eternity and would never have to say goodbye. Ever. It doesn't end here. That is the essence of joy when happiness is nowhere to be found.

I laid my hands on my tiny baby and prayed that either here or in heaven, he would be healed that day. In Jesus' name. We walked to the end of the hallway, guided by the prayers of countless people elsewhere, leaving the ventilator behind. Pat and I sat and held our baby boy, kissing him, admiring him, talking to him. "I want to keep you" was my most honest plea that I whispered to him.

Elizabeth would come in periodically to check his vitals and hook up his feeding syringes. (Sweet thing had been eating through his nose since going on the ventilator hours after birth.) She did her best to provide as many experiences as she could for us with Benjamin. She brought in a cart so that we could give him a bath. We inked his footprints on paper.

She asked if I had any clothes for him that I originally brought with me to the hospital, and somehow, I did. We had not yet been able to clothe him in anything for all the tubes and wires he had been covered in. We slipped him into a Halloween onesie with cute little bats on it and took pictures of him. This was special because phones must be in bags in the NICU, as it is a sterile environment, so we had not been able to take any pictures yet. The nurse got pictures of the two of us with him. We found a surprising amount of comfort in knowing we would be able to do these things with him at least one time, and doing them took the edge off waiting for a sudden decline in his health.

There was one thing that Pat and I just couldn't get over the whole time: "He looks so normal." There was no sign of any struggle. No seizures to speak of. No gasping for air. No turning blue. No stiffness or going completely limp. Most of the time on that day, he was just peacefully sleeping in our arms, like any other newborn baby. At one point, he even opened his eyes and gazed into mine. This was a gift. Having a ventilator on his face had caused swelling around his eyes, so he had not been able to do that up until that point. His eyes were a peaceful sapphire blue. We cherished every moment we could with him, while God told his lungs, "Keep breathing," and his heart, "Keep beating."

To our delighted surprise, it was now getting late at night, and Benjamin was still going strong. The night shift nurses took over and asked if we wanted to sleep for a little while. They promised to wake us promptly if anything changed. I think they wanted to relieve us just as much as they wanted to reexamine him. I'm not sure they counted on him still lasting either.

The next day was Sunday, October 31. That morning, after a couple hours of sleep, we embraced our baby while sipping coffee. He still looked so normal. Doctors made their morning NICU rounds, including meeting with Benjamin. With a full unit, it took some time before a doctor came to speak with us. At about noon, the same doctor who had shed tears while showing us our baby's MRI came to speak with us once more. Her eyes welled with tears yet again as she described Benjamin's evaluation. The outward signs of brain death they had observed yesterday were gone. His vitals were stronger than ever.

"This isn't the same baby. We think he's going to live."

"*Live.*"

A command spoken by an all-powerful God to which His creation obeyed. She was grieved over the trauma we had been through, yet she was speechless as to why Benjamin's condition was so different from what it had been just two days prior. We knew why. While medicine had reached its limit; the Great Physician had not. He has the final say. He has no limits.

In the New Testament, when Jesus laid His hands on people to heal them (or in one case with the hemorrhaging woman, when she reached out and touched Him), the Greek word for "touched" is haptó: "to fasten to, to lay hold of, cling, i.e. (specifically to set on fire—kindle, light." On that Saturday, between sobbing parents, Jesus reached out and touched (haptó) our baby boy. His hand lit a healing fire in Benjamin's tiny body. And like the hemorrhaging woman, the bleeding inside had no choice but to dry up. For the first time since Benjamin was born, tears of unearthly joy streamed down my face.

The good doctor relayed all the hurdles we would encounter over the next days and weeks. The medical team had no projection of what this would mean for Benjamin long term. In fact, with the medically unexplainable having just happened, they were at a loss to tell us anything with certainty, only what scenarios are possible any time there has been brain trauma. Babies who have been deprived of oxygen sometimes have trouble feeding and swallowing once sucking is no longer a reflex, and that was among the first of the challenges that lay ahead. As ridiculous as it is to say, that didn't dampen our spirits in the least.

After she left to attend to his paperwork, we joyously made a FaceTime call to my parents and our daughters at home to proclaim with tears in our eyes that Benjamin had been healed.

"I get to keep you." I beamed, looking down at him.

We promptly were told that the room they had graciously lent us would need to be available should another family need it. As much of a blessing as the space was, we were more than happy to gather our belongings and remove them. A nurse came to walk with us, wheeling Benjamin back to the unit where he was before. I had never thought having a baby in the NICU would bring such a happy feeling. We stayed awhile with him and later went home to be with our other babies to celebrate and to spend some time with them, the panic of being away from Benjamin no longer a factor. We called Broc as well. Call off the funeral!

There are many believers today who, for various reasons, wonder if Jesus still miraculously heals people like He did in the New Testament. I will openly state that despite all my Greek and Hebrew knowledge, I am not a theologian or a pastor, but I will also audaciously say that I can put this thought to rest. He can. He does. He did. I saw it.

5

What's Next

zikkaron (Hebrew): memorial, remembrance, record from Zakar (Hebrew) a memento (or memorable thing, day, writing)

BENJAMIN SPENT THE NEXT 12 DAYS IN THE NICU. Every estimate of when he would go home got pushed back until each specialist was satisfied. What we could expect at home for now remained a giant unknown. With his astonishing turnaround, I wondered if more imaging would reveal a perfectly formed brain. An ultrasound revealed the answer to that question—still an abnormal brain. There was no new bleeding, but there was a large space where the clot had been found, and exactly what was there instead was for now undetermined.

As my daughters later put it, Benjamin had been given a "custom" brain. In Genesis 32, when Jacob wrestles with God, he is given a lifelong limp as a reminder of just how real his encounter was (v.32). Would this space in his brain be something like that? A physical lifelong reminder that God had done something wondrous?

For now, the question seemed to be, God's miraculous healing plus a custom brain equals...? We tried to keep our eyes on God's intervention rather than the list of doctors' speculations. There was no doubt we were in the middle of a miracle, which of course meant we couldn't see the end.

When you don't know how the next chapter will read, it's still jarring as a parent to hear potential scenarios like, "Your son may never walk." Lack of oxygen could mean cerebral palsy, which has its own spectrum of symptoms. An abnormality in this region of the brain could mean an inability to speak or move the left side of his body. It could affect his vision, his behavior, memory, and the list went on and on. On the spectrum of traumatic brain injuries, no two patients are exactly alike. The only things doctors seemed confident in telling us were that his first year of life would be a strong indicator of how things would be in the following years, and the fact that every newborn's brain isn't fully developed at birth would work in his favor.

How were we going to emotionally survive the yearlong wait? Despite my efforts to focus on God, worries about the future crept in uninvited and took root. Would he need a wheelchair someday? Would that mean moving to a new house? Getting a new car? What would happen if he couldn't use the left side of his body once he got too big for me to lift? If he gets to be my husband's size or larger, what then? It was a mental grind every day to drown out the quandary.

One way I tried to combat worry during the long NICU days was to tell Benjamin the stories of Esther, Ehud, and Paul—all Benjamites God had used in mighty ways as I knew He would do with my baby. While the meaning of his name is "son of my right hand," the warriors in the tribe of Benjamin (a militarily strong tribe) were trained to fight left-handed to put their enemies at a disadvantage. With his brain trauma being in the right hemisphere, Benjamin would need to fight to use his left side.

The staff at the hospital did their best to prepare us for taking him home. The transition from his stay was a little overwhelming. We had a very long list of specialists to follow up with, and some of those appointments needed to be arranged before his discharge. Besides regular pediatrician visits, there were meetings with a neurologist, hematologist, and physical therapist; a swallow study; calls with our insurance company and hospital social worker; and so on. He would be on anti-seizure medications leaving the hospital, and the nurses trained us on exactly how to administer those.

Leaving our safety net brought mixed emotions. As much as we wanted to be home with Benjamin, if something went wrong while he was at the hospital, he was surrounded by a team of medical professionals watching every second of the day and night who would be able to respond in seconds. That wouldn't be the case at home. If a neurological event happened, would we know what to do, and could we do it well enough until help arrived?

Besides all the medical care they provided for Benjamin while we were there, so many people did an abundance of things to care for us. They had impacted our lives in such meaningful ways that it was difficult to say goodbye. During the time he was not expected to make it, one of the nurses wanted to make sure we had at least one Halloween picture of him. Sometime when we weren't with him (probably in the middle of the night), she slipped him into a football costume the best she could with all the wires and tubes and got some pictures. She even found time during her shift to make a scrapbook page to go along with it that we could keep.

There was a woman who faithfully came every Tuesday and played the harp for all the babies who were staying there. She had no relation to any of them but still hauled her instrument to and from the hospital to bring them comfort. There were so many things that may seem small but meant the world to us at a time when we were hurting.

Packing with us all the fear and joy that had accumulated over the past two and a half weeks, Pat and I finally took Benjamin home on November 12. We were greeted by beaming smiles as we brought our baby through the door of the home we thought he would never live in.

Our son Sean was just shy of two years old at the time and had been struggling over the past few weeks, not understanding why we had been away from home so much. He was behind with speech and emotional regulation, which would later be confirmed as autism, so we had no idea how he would respond to a new baby suddenly being present. He squealed with delight, curiously peering at this tiny new friend. The best way I can describe his behavior is that he considered himself the proud owner of a new human puppy. Our girls were able to hold their new baby brother, free of wires, tubes, and facemasks.

My parents, who had been the stand-in caretakers, were both overjoyed and past exhausted. Sure, they knew they were making the trip to Texas to help with our new arrival, but they had gone above and beyond the call of duty over the past few weeks, cooking meals, taking the girls to and from school and activities, and caring for Sean all day. They needed some off-duty hours. They had more than earned it.

Our new life as a family of six had some elements that were atypical. We had a strict anti-seizure medication regimen. It was strange how I knew exactly what needed to be done but still felt somewhat unprepared. The nurses had tutored both of us on how things were to be done once we got home, and we did them exactly as we had been taught. That still didn't help the sinking feeling I had in my stomach the first time I administered his oral medication at home via a small baby syringe. Giving my newborn such heavy medication didn't exactly make me feel like mother of the year, necessary as it might be.

Pat and I were both terrified at the thought of leaving Benjamin in his crib to sleep. That first morning of his life, had we kept him in our room as we both slept, he could have easily stopped breathing without us noticing until it was too late. Deciding to have him in the nursery under the watchful eye of the nursing staff was a gift from God that saved him from living only a few hours. Since then, he had been monitored all day and all night in the NICU. It was somewhat of a relief that he now did the normal newborn thing and refused to sleep unless he was cradled in someone's arms.

It was during the middle of one of those nights, Benjamin steadily breathing as he slept in my arms, that I was able to enjoy one of many special moments of remembrance and redemption.

Remembrance is a common thread throughout both the Old and New Testaments. Calling to mind God's faithfulness in the past is what drives us to trust Him in the present. He instructs the Israelites repeatedly as they are traveling through the wilderness, preparing to enter the Promised Land: remember. Remember where you've been delivered from, harrowing as it may be. Remember the narrow place you thought you'd never escape. Remember how God intervened on your behalf. Remember the miraculous things that you prayed longingly and desperately for and how it took your breath away when God came through. Remember the blessings He has bestowed upon you. Remember and pass it on so your children know.

As the Israelites had just set foot on the far side of the Jordan River, closing in on the gap between them and the Promised Land after 40 years in the wilderness, the Lord commanded Joshua to instruct the leaders of the tribes of Israel to go back. Yes, the first thing they were instructed to do after the long-awaited crossing was to go back. Not back into slavery. Not back to wandering. Go back into the Jordan to where the ark of the covenant was, and each take a stone from the parted waters of the river. They were to carry the stones on their shoulders to where they would lodge that night. Why?

> ...so that when your children ask you later, saying 'What do these stones mean to you?' then you shall say to them, 'Because the waters of the Jordan were cut off before the ark of the covenant of the LORD; when it crossed the Jordan, the waters of the Jordan were cut off.' So these stones shall become a memorial to the sons of Israel forever. (Josh. 4:6–7 NASB 1995)

The word for "memorial" in this verse is *zikkaron*—a memorial, remembrance, record, coming from the word *zakar*, a memento (or memorable thing, day, or writing). I love that these stones were chosen simply because they were there when a miracle of God was unfolding. They weren't fancy or costly. A passerby who saw them later, who didn't know the story, would see, well, rocks. Nothing more. But to those who knew, the stones would forever signify that God did an amazing work that brought them into the land He had promised them.

A pen and paper used to record a story can become an enduring memorial testament to what God has done. A hospital wristband kept on a nightstand, a photo, a song on a playlist—the most everyday things can become reminders of a divine rescue. A reminder of the wilderness that you thought you might not make it through.

That night, with my son sound asleep in my arms, I went back. I remembered being alone in a hospital room and thinking things would never be okay. I remembered turning on a movie to silence the quiet that rang in my ears. Now at home, I turned on that same movie. The content of the movie didn't change. To anyone else, it wouldn't seem particularly holy. But in a moment when I had lost hope, and God was doing something miraculous, that movie was playing. Heart overflowing with gratitude, I watched it once more with my son, whom just days ago I feared I would never hold again, snuggled against my chest. A multitude of questions were yet to be answered, but I watched, assured that God is capable of making things *way* more than just okay.

6

New Normal

chul/chuwl (Hebrew): to twist, whirl, dance, writhe, fear, tremble, travail, be in anguish, be pained ... to wait anxiously, to be made to writhe, to be made to bear, to be born ... suffering, torture, to be distressed.

AFTER A WHIRLWIND FIRST FEW WEEKS OF BENJAmin's life, Pat and I were now trying to find a new everyday rhythm as parents of four. The care of a newborn takes on a different tone when that baby has a special, unpredictable need. It was strange to frame coming milestones as "if he walks" or "if he is able to speak" when those are usually given expectations. When a baby who is normally content suddenly cries and fusses for hours, of course, a parent starts to worry that something serious is wrong. But when a child has a serious health condition from the beginning, that worry grows claws and fangs. Completely run-of-the-mill baby things, like gas in his tummy making him crabby, would send me into a panicked frenzy. Terrifying questions would flood my mind. What if he's having swelling in his brain again? What if his oxygen levels are dropping? Should I head to the emergency room?

I'll be honest: There were plenty of times when Benjamin was contentedly sleeping, and I would still find that panic setting in and would just cry. It happened to the point where my husband began to worry that I wasn't allowing myself to bond with Benjamin because I was so caught up in fear.

I'll call myself out on this right here, right now. On a tumultuous road like the one we were on, I could have made things a little easier on myself by reaching out for help. Parents of a child with special circumstances often live in an ongoing state of feeling overwhelmed. I had several people ask if I was getting any kind of counseling for my own well-being.

In the first year of Benjamin's life, we were also figuring things out with our other children, such as my son Sean being autistic. The number of appointments we had to keep between all my kiddos going to doctors, physical therapy, and speech therapy (the list goes on and on) was staggering. We had about 150 appointments on top of regular day-to-day activities that first year. The thought of making *more* appointments and filling out *more* paperwork put me in a state of panic, so I didn't do what I now recommend anyone else do.

Make sure you are looking out for your needs too. Mamas, we all do the same thing. We are willing to jump through any hoop and bulldoze any barrier necessary to care for our babies, but we feel selfish for doing the same for our own needs, and we set them aside, hoping they will just go away. If you're a parent, especially one with a child with special needs, you need to make time for sitting in your heavenly Father's presence and for caring for yourself, whatever that looks like.

As I adjusted to being Benjamin's mom, I had guilt involved in the process too. God had already done miraculous, inexplicable things in Benjamin's first days. So why was so much uncertainty and struggle lurking in my mind? I shouldn't be afraid of the unknown, should I? Was that a lack of faith, and if so, how could I have a lack of faith after all that God had done?

Remember when I said that some words in Hebrew or Greek just paint a brilliant picture? Well, here's a doozy. Put on your word nerd boots. They fit, I promise. I'd be very surprised if this one doesn't blow your mind.

One of the passages I retreat to time and again in Scripture is Psalm 37. It's about struggling on multiple levels. Even if you read the Hebrew word at the beginning of this chapter, you will likely be surprised at how it fits in here. The first part of Psalm 37:7 is an instructive command: "Rest in the Lord and wait patiently for Him." Sounds kind of passive, doesn't it? Peaceful. Quaint. Kind of put together, everything in its place, a place for everything.

Nope.

The word for "wait patiently" is *chul* (or *chuwl*) in Hebrew. Its definition reads, "To twist, whirl, dance, writhe, fear, tremble, travail, be in anguish, be pained ... wait anxiously, to be made to writhe, be made to bear, to be born ... suffering, torture, wait longingly, to be distressed." Bit of a different mental image, isn't it? It's probably a more familiar picture for most of us if we're honest.

Here's the kicker: "Waiting patiently" is a command. It's a command issued by God to engage in this dance with Him. Why in the world? Because that is where relationship with Him happens. He uses this dance to grow us beyond what we thought possible, if we will just be willing to let Him lead, rather than pretend everything is neat and tidy when we approach His throne. Dancing is what happens when we *give* Him whatever it is we are writhing, whirling, bearing, and suffering with, being tortured by, and waiting longingly for, rather than pretending all is well.

Looking deeper at this colorful word, I read on one of my favorite Bible resource sites (studylight.com) that the pain described in this word was at one point commonly associated with a hole drilled by an ancient tool called a bow drill. The term "bow drill" didn't ring any bells, so I did some digging. I found, as the name might suggest, the tool's structure is like a bow used for shooting an arrow, but it's much smaller. The string that is attached at both ends of the bow can be used to twist around a stick. With the stick in one hand, and the bow in the other, the user can pull the string back and forth vigorously on the stick, and eventually, the stick will bore a hole into another surface. Bear in mind that the stick may or may not be especially sharp, so this was a more drawn-out process than drilling a hole with power tools that can do the job in seconds.

But there is another use for this tool that makes the painful picture it paints even more beautiful. The other use—you may have guessed it— is to use the friction to create smoke and even kindle a fire (remember *haptó*?). Just as the same bow can be used for drilling a hole and starting a fire, God can use a piercing, painful circumstance as the tool to start a healing fire. God's kind of fire, in the metaphorical sense. Sometimes God's healing is an instantaneous thing, and sometimes it is a methodical loving process (and yes, it often hurts) as He takes our anguish and replaces it with Himself.

As far as the dance described above, I felt it in full fury walking each day in uncertainty of what my son's condition would look like long term. It simply couldn't be done by strength alone, which seems to be a hallmark of God's calling in story after story. Not only does He invite us to put down our guilt and our fear and dance with Him, but He will also supply the strength we need to do so. Sometimes things can still be scary after something miraculous happens. Dancing is about surrendering that fear to Him rather than clinging to it. Only then can we find the strength to tell fear that it isn't invited.

A somewhat welcome distraction from this dance was all the dates on our calendar that happened back-to-back after our NICU stay. Benjamin came home not long before Thanksgiving. We had abundantly more to be thankful for that year. Between all the scheduled doctor's appointments and the holidays of the season (this is also prime birthday time at our house), we had some kind of hustle going on every day. We had a long list of specialists who wanted to have an initial appointment to see Benjamin.

One thing seemed to be a common denominator with every appointment: the doctor's confused stare as they saw and examined Benjamin for the first time. Whatever they had pictured when reading his case on paper clearly didn't match up with what they were seeing. Their startled confusion was usually followed up with rapid-fire questions about his behavior since coming home from the hospital. The hematologist wanted the most details out of any of the doctors about how our story had gone. After looking at Benjamin, he smiled warmly and said, "There's nothing wrong with your son."

Not all specialists agreed with that. Despite Benjamin being so different from whatever they had pictured, many just wouldn't let go of the worst-case scenario. I know that none of them speculated this way to inspire fear or add stress. They were giving us what was medically most likely, whether that was observable or not. Over-speculation was a storm we were going to need to weather for a long time. It's hard to listen to one professional after another get caught up on things Benjamin "wasn't doing" at the age of one month or two when these concerns were never an issue with our other children.

What was amazing, though, was that every time we went back to another doctor's appointment, each doctor was more and more flabbergasted over what Benjamin could do. We were still doing the recommended things, like weekly physical therapy, but Benjamin just didn't seem to need it. He was knocking milestones out of the park on time, if not early, at each developmental stage. We even got the green light to begin very slowly cutting back on seizure medications.

An element of redemption for Benjamin was the sort of "bucket list" of places to go that we made while holding him in the NICU. We had told him about all the places we wished we could have taken him when we thought we were going to lose him. Even after bringing him home, the concept of traveling away from home was a bit scary at first. If something happened, we would want to be near our doctors, and honestly, I wasn't sure when the idea of travel *wouldn't* be frightening. After about six months of no neurological events, we decided it was time to brave those fears, take that list of things we had wished we could do with him, *and go and do them.*

The first place we wanted to try was the beach. Being in Texas, we thought that might be a good baby step as far as leaving town, as we would not even have to leave the state to find the shoreline. Our family went to Galveston, Texas, and had an absolutely glorious time. With all four of our babies being "neurospicy," we weren't fully sure, especially with our son Sean, if sand and ocean would go over well. But he couldn't get enough! Our teenage girls left all their adolescent worries behind and played freely without a care in the world.

One evening on the beach, I was holding Benjamin and gazing at the water and looking at the majestic colors in the sunset sky. I know that there was no way he could have known, but the way he turned to me, looked into my eyes, and just peacefully smiled made it feel like he knew this was one of the things we told him about when he was hooked to a ventilator, and now he was here, getting to soak it all in. I felt like he knew this was one of a million second chances he would get.

At nine months, Benjamin, or "Benji" as we began calling him, decided he was tired of watching all his older siblings run around and took his first steps. Benjamin was walking. *Walking.* Soon he was not just walking, but running, climbing, jumping, and dancing. Dancing quickly became his favorite thing to do. To this day, when music plays, his little bottom just can't sit still. He has a special place in his heart for harp music, likely thanks to the loving woman whom we have affectionately dubbed "Harp Lady" who visited him faithfully in the NICU.

Milestones are precious with every child—moments when everything changes and new adventures begin. A child's world to explore gets bigger, and so does their understanding of the world around them. With a prognosis as grim and vague as Benjamin's was, those moments aren't only precious—they're victorious. We waited for many moments, like the first time crawling, walking, and talking, unsure if they would ever happen. All of those "He may not ever..." statements, one by one, became a display of what happens when God steps in and redefines what's possible.

I dare say this story has changed that definition for many people both in and outside of the medical field. Family and friends began to mention that they had told other people about Benjamin's story, and how amazed they were. People we would likely never meet were being encouraged by our little guy. The more this happened, the more I realized that God was answering the prayer I had prayed over him before he was born. Inspired by Psalm 71:7, I had prayed that he would be a marvel to many because God was his stronghold and refuge.

On October 27, 2022, exactly a year after the most terrifying day of our lives, we humbly and joyfully celebrated Benjamin's first birthday. This day was one miracle away from being a sorrowful reminder of our son who didn't survive, but instead, it brought jubilee. It was a day that I did not dare picture a year ago as Benji was taken from me to another hospital. I was afraid then to hope that he would last through that night. Now, with family and a house full of shiny mylar balloons, today was Benjamin's big day. It was precious and victorious.

Not long after his first birthday, our pediatric neurologist had further imaging done of Benjamin's brain. In amazement, he showed us the images of the brain, which contained a fluid-filled cyst in a large portion of it (my estimation was that it filled one-fourth of his brain). The lack of brain matter where brain matter would normally be had done absolutely nothing to hinder our son's first-year development. No new bleeding was there, and the old blood from his clot was nowhere to be found. His doctor's assessment was that there was no risk that the fluid would in any way become volatile. It would just remain there, giving Benjamin a "custom" brain.

With Benji still being so young, many developmental milestones have yet to be seen, but the once unnerving questions about what the future will hold just don't carry the authority they once did. Things aren't the same as they were when God first set us out on this journey of expanding our family. They never will be again. But that's the whole point.

Christmas songs, especially those with the word "Noel," still bring tears. Much of the month of December does. We have lost many hours of sleep and cried many tears since losing Blake and having Sean and Benjamin. We have learned a humbling lesson or two about raising neurodivergent children. I'm pretty sure I age in dog years now (hopefully that slows down). Benjamin's brain will never look like yours or mine because God had a bigger picture in mind than "normal" for how He made our son.

The answers to lingering questions don't matter as much as the fact that God has a clear outcome in mind for the lifelong miracle that is unfolding in our lives. These past few years have been the turbulent first chapter for Benjamin, and despite the tears, the grumbling, the doubts, and the fear, just like the Israelites in the wilderness, not for a moment did we go it alone.

7

The Good Shepherd

oudeís (Greek): no one, nothing at all ... is a powerful negating conjunction. It rules out by definition, i.e. "shuts the door" objectively and leaves no exceptions.... Oudeís is deductive in force, so it excludes every (any) example ... categorically excludes declaring as fact that no valid example exists.

IN CASE YOU SKIPPED OVER THE INTRODUCTION AT THE beginning of this book (no judgment here), I want to state again that this final chapter is a little different from the rest of the book. I've wrapped up my story as a mama with my babies. I count it a genuine pleasure to have invited you into my story, and hopefully, some of the previous and following words impact yours. This final chapter takes a broader look at infant loss. I stated earlier my hope in writing this story is that it becomes a comfort, especially to those who have been through something similar.

I know the reason you may be reading this book is because you have been through infant loss or loss of another kind. I am profoundly so sorry for what you have been through. One of the downsides to writing is that I can't sit down next to you and hear your story. I wish we could share coffee or tea, and I would let you say (or not say) what is on your heart. Sadly, the topic of infant loss gets side-stepped, both in and outside of the church. If you have been ignored during your loss, I am genuinely sorry. I want to assure you that you are both seen and heard by your heavenly Father (Isa. 59:1, Ps. 34:18).

By no means do I believe that the following pages will put to rest every question and doubt that arises with infant loss. It is my hope, however, to provide truth that God gives us as a resting place for grieving hearts. That's why at the end of each statement, I added the words "rest in that." I hope you will do that for as long as your heart needs.

Words of man fall short on matters like these. Only words from God have the power to bring healing at its deepest level. That is why, for each claim I made, I point to a specific verse or specific verses in scripture, rather than offering additional arguments or thoughts of my own, though they might further my point. Some statements are simple, and some get a bit wordy to fully explain.

I know wordiness is not always the best way to comfort someone who has been through a loss; in fact, at some stages in grief, it's best not to say anything at all. If your heart is not ready to receive these or other words, I encourage you to come back when you're ready. Your heavenly Father will patiently wait.

As Christ followers, we believe that accepting the fact that you have sin in your heart (like all human beings) and believing in the death and resurrection of Jesus, God's Son, is how you become forgiven for that sin and enter a life-giving relationship with Him. This faith also makes a way for us to be in heaven with Him for eternity once we leave this earth (John 3:16–18, Rom. 6:23, Eph. 2:8–9, Acts 4:12, John 14:6, Rom. 10:9–10, Heb. 7:25). One of the obvious questions believers (and non-believers) wrestle with then is what about those who have not had the chance to make that decision (such as the unborn, stillborn, or infants who have died). This question leads parents like me to ask, "Where is my baby now?"

A keyword search of miscarriage/stillbirth within scripture doesn't give much to go on, and it would be easy to conclude that the Bible has precious little to say on the matter. The words miscarried/stillborn only appear about six times in scripture (the number of times may be affected by which translation you're looking at), and in five of those cases, it is simply used as a metaphor and doesn't refer to an infant loss event at all (Num. 12:12, Exod. 23:26, Job 3:16, Ps. 58:8, Eccl. 6:3).

While we walked through our loss, God lovingly spoke the following words of comfort over me as I sought Him. He showed me that scripture isn't silent to this kind or any other kind of loss. I fully believe the more comprehensive answer God gives us lies in Himself and the person of Jesus, His Son, revealed to all.

Jesus Abolished Death

> *I am the Living One; I was dead, and now look, I am alive for ever and ever! And I hold the keys of death and Hades.*
>
> —Revelation 1:18 NIV

> *And God raised him [Jesus] up, loosing the pangs of death, because it was not possible for him to be held by it.*
>
> —Acts 2:24 ESV

Through His resurrection, Jesus abolished death and holds the keys to death and Hades. There is no asterisk next to the word "death" in this verse or any other. Jesus' sacrifice has rendered death helpless in every case; it no longer has the final say. No form of death, including infant death, remains supreme over what He has done. Rest in that.

God Is Omniscient

> *Great is our Lord and mighty in power; his understanding has no limit.*
>
> —Psalm 147:5 NIV

> *Nothing in all creation is hidden from God's sight. Everything is uncovered and laid bare before the eyes of him to whom we must give account.*
>
> —Hebrews 4:13 NIV

> *[F]or whenever our heart condemns us, God is greater than our heart, and he knows everything.*
>
> —1 John 3:20 ESV

God is all-knowing, and His plan of salvation has no shortcomings. Miscarriage, stillbirth, and infant death are not an oversight, afterthought, or flaw in His plan of salvation. Rest in that.

God Is Omnipotent

Ah, Lord GOD! It is you who have made the heavens and earth by your great power and by your outstretched arm! Nothing is too hard for you.

—Jeremiah 32:17 ESV

Behold, the LORD's hand is not shortened, that it cannot save, or his ear dull, that it cannot hear.

—Isaiah 59:1 ESV

Because God is an all-powerful God, nothing is too difficult for Him. I know that this point can feel more like a double-edged sword. When His plan of salvation for a child does not include more time for them on this side of eternity, it is a bitter and difficult plan to accept. Even when our understanding falls short, His power (and compassion) does not. Your baby being beyond medicine's ability to save does not mean your baby was beyond God's ability to save. He does not lack power to save anyone and hears the cries of everyone. Rest in that.

God Is All-Seeing

For you formed my inward parts; you knitted me together in my mother's womb. I praise you, for I am fearfully and wonderfully made. Wonderful are your works; my soul knows it very well. My frame was not hidden from you, when I was being made in secret, intricately woven in the depths of the earth."

—Psalm 139:13–15 ESV

Nothing in all creation is hidden from God's sight. Everything is uncovered and laid bare before the eyes of him to whom we must give account.

—Hebrews 4:13 NIV

Unborn babies may be hidden from the world, but they are not hidden from God. He is not only aware of them, but His very presence is also with them, and He intimately wove them together. Yes, He was with your baby and holding them in His hands when they left this world. While a grieving parent may be left with aching empty arms, God's arms are not empty. Rest in that.

He Cherishes His Children

People were also bringing babies to Jesus for him to place his hands on them. When the disciples saw this, they rebuked them. But Jesus called the children to him and said, "Let the little children come to me,

The Good Shepherd

and do not hinder them, for the kingdom of God belongs to such as these."

—Luke 18:15–16 NIV

Infants are precious to Him. While Jesus was here on earth, He scolded His disciples for trying to prevent little children from coming to Him. I'm going to toss a few Greek words in here, because, as a parent, these words spoke volumes to me.

"And they were bringing even their babies to Him..." (v.15). The word "babies" here is *"brephos"* in Greek, meaning an unborn or newborn child (Bible Hub). This word means newborn and unborn.

"Let the little children (*paidion* in Greek, also meaning infant or very little child) come to me, and do not hinder them, for the kingdom of God belongs to such as these" (v.16 NIV). *Belongs to.* That word, in case you were wondering, is *"eimi,"* which is "'straightforward' being *without explicit limits"* (emphasis mine, Bible Hub). Jesus states that the kingdom of God belongs to, without explicit limits, the *brephos* and the *paidion* (infants and little children) of the kingdom. Rest in that.

One of the "I Am" names Jesus proclaims during His time on earth is the Good Shepherd. In the picture that "I Am" statement paints, we are then the sheep He tenderly cares for. In John 10:27–30, Jesus states:

> My sheep hear my voice, and I know them, and they follow me. I give them eternal life, and they will never perish, and no one will snatch them out of my hand. My Father, who has given them to me, is greater than all, and no one is able to snatch them

out of the Father's hand. I and the Father are one. (ESV)

Indulge me in a Greek word one more time because it's a powerful one. Hang in there, and I think you'll be overjoyed you did.

I'm going to fully restate the word definition at the beginning of the chapter because I am that passionate about you not missing it. The word for "no one" used in verse 29 (for "*no one* is able to snatch them out of the Father's hand") is "*oudeís*" in the Greek. The HELPS Word Studies states:

> *oudeís* ... is a powerful negating conjunction. It rules out *by definition*, i.e. "shuts the door" *objectively* and leaves no exceptions.... (*oudeís*) is *deductive* in force so it excludes *every (any) example*.... [It] *categorically excludes*, declaring as a *fact* that no valid example exists. (Bible Hub, Strongs, HELPS Word Studies)

Forgive the wordiness and just let it sink in; if you are in God's hands (remember Psalm 139:13–15), nothing in existence can steal you away from Him. There are no valid examples. Nothing has that power. Including infant death. I remember how helpless it felt to realize that my baby, whom I had not physically miscarried yet, had left without me even knowing when exactly it happened. My baby was gone before I could even say goodbye. "Snatched" would aptly describe how that felt. But no one and nothing snatches anything from our heavenly Father. My baby and yours have never left His hands. Rest in that.

God Offers Forgiveness

I will also say this because sometimes in this context, a loss is not natural but chosen and then deeply regretted. There is forgiveness, and God's forgiveness is sufficient. Rest in that.

> If we confess our sins, he is faithful and just to forgive our sins and to cleanse us from all unrighteousness. (1 John 1:9 ESV)

God Has All Authority

We as believers take certain steps in this life as acts of obedience, submission, and worship. Things like communion and baptism are beautiful examples of these things. Sometimes, though, we can get too attached to customs and believe that someone who never got the chance (or never took the chance) to follow in these ways is beyond God's ability to save. Jesus is not hindered by this. He is powerful enough and has the authority to save those who have not partaken in these elements of faith. Rest in that.

> One of the criminals who were hanged [on a cross] railed at him, saying, "Are you not the Christ? Save yourself and us!" But the other rebuked him, saying, "Do you not fear God, since you are under the same sentence of condemnation? And we indeed justly, for we are receiving the due reward of our deeds; but this man has done nothing wrong." And he said, "Jesus, remember me when you come into your kingdom." And [Jesus] said to him, "Truly, I say to you, today you will be with me in paradise." (Luke 23:39–43 ESV)

This Isn't the End

This fallen world is broken and full of sorrow. When we lose someone we love, we are never quite the same. Grief may not be as raw or visceral with time, but the scars remain. Thankfully, this world is not our home. Not forever, anyway. There will be a new heaven and a new earth. Someday, you will stand in your Savior's presence, and finally, for all time, He will wipe away every tear from your eyes. There will no longer be any death, mourning, or crying. Those things will finally die. Rest in that.

> He will wipe every tear from their eyes, and death shall be no more, neither shall there be mourning, nor crying, nor pain anymore, for the former things have passed away. (Rev. 21:4 ESV)

I know my story is nothing if not emotional, and perhaps the scripture passages listed are emotional for you too. I'm so grateful to you for persevering, even if reading has been difficult for you, and allowing me to share my family's joyous mountain-top experiences of Sean's birth and Benjamin's healing as well as the sorrow of losing Blake and nearly losing Benjamin.

Perhaps your own story reflects some of the same elements, or reading has brought to mind other painful circumstances you have gone through. I could have no higher hope than for our story to encourage you in the story God is writing in your life. You just may find yourself somewhere inside a miracle as well.

My ending prayer for you is the same one I prayed over Benjamin before he was born on an ordinary day in a car line.

I pray that you will become a marvel to many because God is your strong refuge (Ps. 71:7).

References

Blake

Luke 24:15 Greek Transliteration. BibleHub.com.

Strong's Concordance. Greek 1448 *eggizó*. BibleHub.com.

HELPS Word Studies. Copyright 2021 by Discovery Bible. Strong's Greek 1448 *eggizó*. Biblehub.com

NAS Exhaustive Concordance. NAS Exhaustive Concordance of the Bible with Hebrew-Aramaic and Greek Dictionaries. Copyright 1981, 1998 by The Lockman Foundation. All rights reserved, Lockman.org. Eggizo Word origin. BibleHub.com.

October 27

NASB Lexicon Strong's Concordance. Strong's Exhaustive Concordance, Strong's 215 Greek *alalétos*, Strong's 4726 *stenagmos*, Strong's 4727 Greek *stenazó*. BibleHub.com.

NAS Exhaustive Concordance of the Bible with Hebrew-Aramaic and Greek Dictionaries. Copyright 1981, 1998 by the Lockman Foundation. Lockman.org. 215 Greek *alalétos*, Strong's 4726 Greek *stenagmos*, Strong's 4727 *stenazó*. BibleHub.com.

"Thayer's Expanded Greek Definition, Electronic Database." Bible Lexicon Strong's Greek *alalétos*. Copyright 2002, 2003, 2006, 2011 by Biblesoft, Inc. Biblesoft.com. StudyLight.org.

Little Hope

NASB Lexicon Strong's Concordance. Strong's Hebrew 6757 *tsalmaveth*. BibleHub.com.

Bible Lexicon Brown-Driver-Briggs. Strong's Hebrew 6757 *tsalmaveth*. Studylight.org

The Miracle

NASB Lexicon Strong's Concordance. Strong's Exhaustive Concordance. Strong's Greek 681 *haptó*. BibleHub.com.

NAS Exhaustive Concordance. NAS Exhaustive Concordance of the Bible with Hebrew-Aramaic and Greek Dictionaries. Copyright 1981, 1998 by the Lockman Foundation. Lockman.org. Strong's Greek 681 *haptó*. BibleHub.com.

Thayer's Expanded Greek Definition, Electronic Database Bible Lexicon Strong's Greek 681 *haptó*. StudyLight.org. Copyright 2001–2022.

What's Next

NASB Lexicon. Strong's Hebrew 2146 *zikkaron*. BibleHub.com.

NAS Exhaustive Concordance. NAS Exhaustive Concordance of the Bible with Hebrew-Aramaic and Greek

References

Dictionaries. Copyright 1981, 1998 by the Lockman Foundation. Lockman.org. Strong's Hebrew 2146 BibleHub.com.

Bible Lexicon Brown-Driver-Briggs'. Strong's Hebrew 2146 *zikkaron*. StudyLight.org.

Gill, John. *Gill's Exposition of the Entire Bible* (Judges 20:16). Exposition of the Entire Bible by John Gill [1746-63]. Text courtesy of Sacred Texts Archive. BibleHub.com. Judges 20:16 Commentary.

"What does Judges 20:16 Mean?" Bibleref.com. Copyright 2002–2024.

New Normal

NASB Lexicon Strong's Concordance. Strong's Exhaustive Concordance Strong's Hebrew 2342. BibleHub.com.

Bible Lexicon Brown-Driver-Briggs. Strong's 2342 Hebrew *chul*. "Ancient Hebrew Lexicon Definitions." AHL Definitions Copyright: 1999–2024. Jeff Benner, Ancient Hebrew Research Center. Studylight.com.

The Good Shepherd

Strong's Concordance. Strong's Greek 3762 *oudeís* and *outheís, oudemia, ouden* and *outhen*. BibleHub.com

Strong's Exhaustive Concordance. 3762 *oudeís* and *outheís, oudemia, ouden* and *outhen* BibleHub.com.

"HELPS Word Studies." Copyright 2021 by Discovery Bible. Strong's Greek 3762 *oudeís*. BibleHub.com.

NAS Exhaustive Concordance of the Bible with Hebrew-Aramaic and Greek Dictionaries. Copyright 1981, 1998 by the Lockman Foundation. *Oudeís* word origin. BibleHub.com.

Biblegateway.com. The Zondervan Corporation. Keywords "miscarriage," "stillbirth." Numbers 12:12, Exodus 23:26, Job 3:16, Psalm 58:8, Ecclesiastes 6:3 (2x) (sources for keyword search of miscarriage, stillbirth, stillborn, etc. in scripture)

Made in the USA
Middletown, DE
16 February 2025